Tom Brady

Heart of the Huddle

By
MARK STEWART

THE MILLBROOK PRESS
BROOKFIELD, CONNECTICUT

M

THE MILLBROOK PRESS

Produced by
BITTERSWEET PUBLISHING
John Sammis, President
and
TEAM STEWART, INC.
RESEARCHED AND EDITED BY MIKE KENNEDY

Series Design and Electronic Page Makeup by
JAFFE ENTERPRISES
Ron Jaffe

All photos courtesy AP/Wide World Photos, Inc., except the following:
Rob Tringali Jr., SportsChrome — Cover
Junipero Serra High School — Pages 7, 8
AP/WWP/South Bend Tribune — Page 15 top
The following images are from the collection of Team Stewart:
Leaf Inc. © 1990 — Page 9 top
Topps Chewing Gum © 1962 — Page 9 middle
Action Packed, Inc. © 1994 — Page 9 bottom
The Topps Company, Inc. © 2000 — Page 20
Fleer/Skybox International LP © 2002 — Page 23 top left
Sports Illustrated for Kids/TIME Inc. © 2002 — Page 25
Primedia, Inc. © 2001 — Page 33
ESPN © 2001 — Page 38 bottom right
Sports Illustrated/TIME Inc. © 2002 — Page 43

Printed in the United States of America

Published by
The Millbrook Press, Inc.
2 Old New Milford Road
Brookfield, Connecticut   06804
www.millbrookpress.com

Library of Congress Cataloging-in-Publication Data

Stewart, Mark.
  Tom Brady : heart of the huddle / by Mark Stewart.
    p. cm. — (Football's new wave)
  Includes index.
  Summary: A biography of the New England Patriots star quarterback who led
his team to win Super Bowl XXVI.
  ISBN 0-7613-2907-2 (lib. bdg.) — ISBN 0-7613-1929-8 (pbk.)
  1. Brady, Tom, 1977—Juvenile literature. 2. Football
players--United States—Biography—Juvenile literature. [1. Brady, Tom, 1977-
2. Football players.] I. Title: Heart of the huddle. II. Title. III. Series.
  GV939.B685 S74 2003
  618.1'75—dc21
                                                        2002014112

         lib: 1 3 5 7 9 10 8 6 4 2
         pbk: 1 3 5 7 9 10 8 6 4 2

Contents

Tale of the Tortoise

chapter 1

> *"I am not a person that's self-satisfied just being out there. I want to go out there and play great."*
>
> —TOM BRADY

By the time you reach your twenty-first birthday, you will probably hear the words "be prepared" a thousand times. What you make of that message is up to you. Tom Brady made a career out of it. At every stage of his life, he has been ready to take advantage of an opportunity. Along the way he has won the praise and admiration of millions of football fans, and turned his biggest doubters into true believers.

Tom was born on August 3, 1977, in San Mateo, California. San Mateo is a suburban community outside of San Francisco, with a population just under 100,000. Tom Sr. was a banker who made a good living. His wife, Galynn, stayed at home and took care of Tom and his three older sisters, Maureen, Julie, and Nancy. The Bradys were big

Tom soaks up the love during the New England Patriots' victory parade in February 2002. By always being prepared, he was able to beat the odds and win big games at each level of his football career—including the Super Bowl!

Candlestick Park, where Tom and his family attended many baseball and football games.

sports fans. The kids enjoyed a wide range of athletics, and their parents took them often to Candlestick Park, where the Giants played baseball and the 49ers played football.

Among the hometown stars Tom rooted for were Will Clark and Bob Brenly of the Giants, and Jerry Rice and Joe Montana of the 49ers. Tom's first sports memory, in fact, took place during the 1981 National Football Conference championship game between the 49ers and Dallas Cowboys. Tom's dad got tickets to the game and took him along. The four-year-old cried for the entire first half, but not because his beloved 49ers were fighting for their lives. He was furious at his parents for refusing to buy him one of those big foam "We're #1" hands!

Tom has fonder memories of the second half. He was mesmerized by Montana, who guided the underdog 49ers to a dramatic comeback, which was capped off by a touchdown pass to Dwight Clark in the back of the end zone. The victory tipped the balance of power in pro football, and made Tom a lifelong fan of Joe Montana. It was shortly after this experience that he told his friends and relatives what he wanted to do with his life: play pro football.

There was little in those early years to suggest Tom would fulfill this dream. In neighborhood

Joe Montana, Tom's hero since he was four

games he was never the best player, and he would get wiped out in foot races against the fastest boy on his block. Undaunted, Tom kept challenging the kid. Each time he lost, he tried to think of some small improvement he could make that would get him a couple of inches closer. "Every day he'd kill me," Tom remembers. "I'd challenge him again and he'd kill me again. I kept challenging him until finally I beat him. It was kind of like the tortoise and the hare. I was the tortoise."

Tom got some of his competitive fire from his sisters, who also hated to lose. Maureen, Julie, and Nancy were all good athletes, and the competition regularly spilled into the living room. Battles over the remote control (the girls liked soap operas and Tom didn't) were legendary. "We doted on him, but that only lasted for so long," Julie remembers. "We used to compete for absolutely everything, and we pushed him all the time."

BEST ATHLETE: TOM BRADY

The star of the Serra High baseball and football teams, Tom was voted his school's best athlete.

Forced to rely on his wits both at home and on the playing field, Tom naturally gravitated to positions that rewarded his analytical skills. Despite his football ambitions, Tom's best sport was baseball. From Little League right through high school he was an excellent hitter with a powerful arm and an exceptional head for the game. In the end, he settled in at catcher, where his combination of intelligence and athleticism attracted the attention of Major League scouts. Tom loved playing catcher. Crouching behind home plate, handling the pitchers, setting the defense, figuring out hitters' weaknesses—he felt he was in total control of the game.

Tom's quarterbacking career was limited to touch football games until he enrolled at Junipero Serra High School, an all-boys Catholic school in San Mateo. The school had terrific sports teams, so he knew it would take a while to win a starting job. Tom studied the playbook, learned the strengths and weaknesses of his teammates in

Thomas E. Brady Jr.
If you want to play with the big boys, you gotta learn how to play in the tall grass. Family I love you all. FB 1-4; BKB 1-2; BSB 1-4; BLOCK 4; JSA 2; TRIVIA 1-4; FRIAR

Jero
I'm Just A
Book Of
thor. Tha
MariaHe
FB 1-2 4
CREW 3

Tom looks dashing in his high school yearbook photo.

practice, and imagined himself succeeding in game situations so he would be ready to produce if called upon. "If you want to be a great player, you've got to put the work in," he says.

Tom's big chance came in 1992, during his sophomore year, when the number-one quarterback on the junior varsity was injured. Tom took command of the team and impressed everyone with his leadership abilities. The mistakes he made were mostly from inexperience, and he rarely made the same mistake twice. After the season, the varsity coach, Tom MacKenzie, took Tom aside and said he would give him a chance to win the starting job on the varsity in 1993.

Tom came to tryouts in 1993 and blew away the competition. He had gained confidence as the school's star catcher the previous spring, and worked like a madman to get his mind and body ready for the football season. He walked and talked and looked like the starter from the first day—and coaches and teammates began treating him that way. When Tom showed he could execute every play in the team's book, Coach MacKenzie's choice was a no-brainer.

Tom felt that no one on the team should be asked to do something that he couldn't do. This philosophy spilled over into the team's workout regimen, which Tom ramped up with a jump-rope routine that improved everyone's footwork and timing. Between his junior and senior years, he invited his teammates to join him in a grueling conditioning program that he had designed. He got very few takers. But he did earn their respect—a crucial element in

Did You Know?

Tom would have had a difficult time making the majors as an Expo. In the same draft, Montreal took two other catchers, Michael Barrett and Brian Schneider. They formed the team's catching corps during the 2001 and 2002 seasons.

SERRA SUPERSTARS

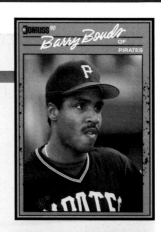

Tom is not the only star athlete to attend Junipero Serra High School. In fact, you could start quite a card collection just starting with the school's All-Star alumni!

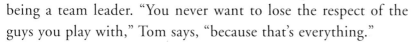

PLAYER	ACHIEVEMENT
BARRY BONDS	HOME RUN KING
LYNN SWANN	YOUNGEST SUPER BOWL MVP (AGE 23) AND 2002 HALL OF FAMER
JIM FREGOSI	6-TIME ALL-STAR SHORTSTOP (1960s & 70s) AND PENNANT-WINNING MANAGER (1993)
GREGG JEFFERIES	TWO-TIME ALL-STAR (1990s)
DANNY FRISELLA	MEMBER OF 1969 MIRACLE METS
JOHN ROBINSON	LEGENDARY USC FOOTBALL COACH
TIM CULLEN	TOP FIELDING SECOND BASEMAN IN AL (1970)
DAN SERAFINI	FIRST-ROUND DRAFT CHOICE BY MINNESOTA TWINS

being a team leader. "You never want to lose the respect of the guys you play with," Tom says, "because that's everything."

All that preparation paid off during Tom's two varsity seasons. He completed 236 of 447 passes for 3,702 yards and 31 touchdowns in 1993 and 1994. In his senior year he was honored as an All-American by *Blue Chip Illustrated* and *Prep Football Report*. He also earned recognition as an All-State and All-Far West quarterback.

Yet for all of his accomplishments on the gridiron, Tom's future still seemed to be on the baseball diamond. He was selected by the Montreal Expos in the 1994 Major League draft. The Expos were baseball's hottest young team at the time, and it was very tempting to accept their offer. But he also was being recruited by several big-time college football programs around the country. Tom talked it over with his parents and decided to stick with his dream of being a pro quarterback. Although the odds looked better in baseball, he was not ready to let football go.

Stuck on the Sidelines

chapter 1

"The coach decides who plays, and when he says to go in there, you play your butt off."

—TOM BRADY

Tom accepted a scholarship from the University of Michigan. Lloyd Carr, the team's new head coach, decided to red-shirt him for the 1995 season, meaning Tom could practice with the team but was not eligible to play. This would give him a year to learn the offense without losing a year of eligibility. Tom watched from the sidelines as freshman Scott Driesbach and sophomore Brian Griese battled for the starting quarterback job. Neither was able to nail it down, but the Wolverines' defense was strong enough to get the team to the Alamo Bowl.

Tom really had to prove himself to Michigan coach Lloyd Carr. It took three years to win the starting job.

Brian Griese, the man who blocked Tom's path until 1998

In 1996, Tom won the third-string job, as the top slot continued to seesaw between Driesbach and Griese. Tom saw little action, however, getting into just two games. He completed 3 of 5 passes for 26 yards. Once again, the defense came through and Michigan won enough games to earn a post-season appearance. Griese led the Wolverines to a 41–14 win over Auburn in the Outback Bowl.

When tryouts began in 1997, Griese and Driesbach once again locked horns for the starting quarterback job. To their surprise, the best passer in camp ended up being Tom. He was certain that he had earned the number-one job. But Coach Carr decided to hand the reins over to Griese. Tom was furious. Hadn't he done everything to earn the job? Hadn't he studied enough films and taken enough snaps in practice to gain the coach's confidence? Tom was so disappointed that he started to do

"He wasn't the greatest athlete, but he was the smartest guy on the field, and he prided himself on knowing everything that was happening on the field."

—IAN GOLD, COLLEGE TEAMMATE

The Wolverine offense fed off its defense, which was led by Heisman Trophy winner Charles Woodson.

something he had never done before: complain.

"I turned into a whiner," he admits. "Nothing was my fault, and finally I told Coach Carr that I wanted to transfer to Cal [the University of California]. He said, 'Just put everything else out of your mind and worry about making yourself better.' He was right."

Coach Carr was also right about Griese. The offense seemed to relax with the senior in charge. Meanwhile, Michigan's defense dominated from the season's opening kickoff. Charles Woodson, the star cornerback, shut down half the field himself. He also helped out on offense, providing another deep threat to the wide receiver. The Wolverines went undefeated during the regular season, including a perfect 8–0 mark in the Big Ten Conference. This set up a showdown with Washington State in the prestigious Rose Bowl. With Griese leading

> *"You want to be decisive. You want to make good throws. If you're tentative, you're not successful. I've learned that the hard way."*
> —**TOM BRADY**

the way, Carr's troops won, 21–16, and earned a share of the national championship with Nebraska. It was the school's first title since 1948.

For Tom, the 1997 season had its highs and lows. Early in the year, he saw some action and played well, completing 12 of 15 passes. Then in October Tom was rushed to the hospital with appendicitis. He was fine after surgery, but did not play again. The downtime turned out to be helpful. Tom thought back to the kind of team player he had been in high school. He was always the guy who picked up teammates when they were down, who helped boost their confidence. And if a guy was acting like a jerk, well, Tom told him so. Tom realized that *he* had been acting like a jerk. He decided to stay at Michigan, keep his mouth shut, and try to win the starting job in 1998.

Super Starter

"He has that warrior mentality."

—TEAMMATE CLARENCE WILLIAMS

With Brian Griese graduated and Scott Driesbach better suited to being a substitute, the Wolverines were in dire need of a take-charge player at quarterback in 1998. Buoyed by his new attitude and infused with newfound confidence, Tom was zipping beautiful spirals to his receivers and barking out plays in the huddle like a leader. When Coach Carr announced that Tom had earned the starting job, the Michigan players applauded the move.

Tom would have his work cut out for him. Michigan's 1998 schedule—already one of the toughest in the nation—would be even tougher because now everyone would be gunning for the champion Wolverines. No one was worried about the defense; this was one

Did You Know?

In 1998, Tom set school records with 31 completions and 375 passing yards in a loss to archrival Ohio State.

*Notre Dame Stadium,
site of Tom's "sneak preview"*

of the toughest units in college ball. But an offense led by "unknown" Tom Brady had some fans worried. Coach Carr insisted to reporters that Tom had the right stuff, but Tom knew he would have to get off to a good start.

Before school began, Tom took a secret trip. He drove to South Bend, Indiana, where Michigan was scheduled to play its season opener, against Notre Dame. Tom knew that many a young quarterback had been psyched out playing in this historic venue, so he decided to give himself a sneak preview. He literally sneaked into Notre Dame Stadium, and stood on the field soaking it all in for more than an hour. When Tom was ready to leave, he realized the only way out was over a 15-foot (4.5-m) wall. How, he wondered, could he ever explain breaking an arm or ankle under these circumstances? Then he got an idea. "I broke into a maintenance closet, found an extension ladder, threw the thing over the fence and climbed down," Tom laughs.

Tom was not laughing two weeks later, when the Fighting Irish beat the Wolverines. And he was downright angry after losing to Syracuse a week after that. Sensing this was the make-or-break point

*Tom is in command as
Michigan's starting quarterback.*

Tom unloads against Penn State in a 1998 game. The Wolverines won, 27–0.

Before going to the pros, Jim Harbaugh set many of the records Tom broke.

for Michigan's season (and possibly his football career!) Tom pulled his teammates together and talked about what they needed to do to win. The blockers had to work together more, the runners had to trust that the holes would be there, and the receivers had to run crisper routes.

The Wolverines hit the field with renewed spirit and beat Indiana, Minnesota, and Penn State. In fact, they won all but one of their remaining games. Tom played beautifully, completing over 60 percent of his passes and throwing for more yards than any Michigan quarterback since Jim Harbaugh. The team tied for the Big Ten championship, and got a bid to the Citrus Bowl. In that game, Tom engineered a thrilling comeback against the Arkansas Razorbacks.

As the 1999 season opened, Tom knew he could not rest on his accomplishments. In a powerhouse football program like Michigan's, there is always another quarterback breathing down your neck. In this case, his name was Drew Henson. He was regarded as a once-in-a-lifetime talent, and Coach Carr was tempted to give him Tom's job. A great all-around athlete, Henson had been signed to a baseball contract by the Yankees and was thinking about quitting football. Coach Carr promised the youngster that he

Drew Henson (7), Jason Kapsner (13), and Tom (10) pose for the camera during summer practice in 1999. Tom and Drew were battling it out for the starting job.

would play him in the opener against Notre Dame. If he did better than Tom, he would get the starting job.

A couple of years earlier, Tom would have gone ballistic upon hearing such news. But he had learned a valuable lesson about holding his tougue and letting his play speak for itself. In the Notre Dame game, Tom played the first quarter and led the Wolverines to two field goals. Henson played the second quarter and did well, too. However, with the Fighting Irish ahead, Coach Carr and his staff decided that they had to pick one quarterback and let him go the rest of the game. They selected Tom, who rewarded their faith by leading Michigan to a dramatic fourth-quarter victory.

Henson continued to see playing time in Michigan's meetings with Wisconsin, Purdue, and Michigan State, but Tom outgunned him in each game. After a 300-yard

college *stats*

Season	Team	G	Att	Comp	Comp %	Yds	TDs
1996	Michigan	2	4	2	50.0	26	0
1997	Michigan	4	15	12	80.0	103	0
1998	Michigan	13	350	214	61.1	2,636	15
1999	Michigan	12	341	214	62.8	2,586	20
Total		31	710	442	62.3	5,351	35

college *achievements*

Record 4 TDs & 369 Yards in Orange Bowl 2000
All-Big Ten (2nd Team) 1999
Academic All-Big Ten 1998

performance against Illinois, Coach Carr finally made it official: Tom would be the number-one quarterback the rest of the way. Michigan swept through the rest of the schedule and earned a berth in the Orange Bowl against Alabama.

This was Tom's final college game. With 70,000 screaming fans in the stands, the Wolverines and Crimson Tide engaged in an unforgettable aerial battle that saw Tom complete 34 of 46 passes for 369 yards. Four of those passes found receiver David Terrell in the end zone, as Michigan erased a 14-point deficit to force the game into overtime. Tom engineered a scoring drive on the Wolverines' first possession, hitting Shawn Thompson with a 25-yard touchdown pass. Alabama answered with a touchdown of its own, but missed the extra point. Michigan had a 35–34 victory. It was a great way to cap off his college career.

Tom fires a touchdown pass to David Terrell during the final game of his college career.

Fourth-String Follies

chapter 4

> *" Sixth round?*
> *Are you kidding me!"*
> —TOM BRADY

om's numbers as a senior were exceptional. He connected on 214 of 341 attempts for 2,586 yards and 20 touchdowns, while throwing a mere 6 interceptions. His leadership skills were unquestioned, and he had a marvelous head for the game. But NFL scouts had their doubts about Tom.

Yes, he possessed the "intangibles" all teams looked for, but they came wrapped in an unimpressive physical package. Tom was

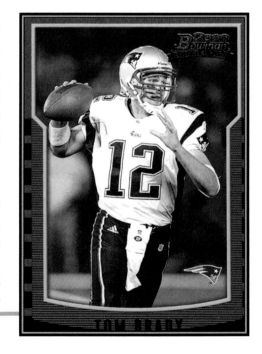

Tom looks confident on his NFL rookie card. "If you're tentative, you're not successful," he says. "I've learned that the hard way."

Coach Bill Belichick in his days as a defensive coordinator with the Jets. The Patriots hired him as head coach hoping he would improve the defense.

not quick enough to elude pro pass rushers, nor did he have the arm strength to "stretch the field" and keep defenses honest by throwing long bombs. His body was a problem, too. Tom stood 6–4 (193 cm), which was fine, but weighed less than 200 pounds (91 kg), which was not. Tom had the makings of a decent backup, but no one believed he would ever be a first-rate starter.

Bill Belichick was in the market for a decent backup. The New England Patriots coach had one of the game's best starters in Drew Bledsoe, but behind him were aging John Friesz and young Michael Bishop, who had failed to mature in his two years with the team. Belichick liked guys who were strong-minded and who refused to back down from a challenge. He felt Tom was this kind of player, and grabbed him in the next-to-last round of the NFL draft.

Tom knew he was not a highly regarded prospect, but he never imagined he would drop so low in the draft. He watched the proceedings with growing frustration at his

The Pats drafted Arizona State star J.R. Redmond three rounds before picking Tom. They would team up to make history one season later.

parents' home. At one point he grabbed a baseball bat and stormed into the backyard. As his father later put it, Tom did a little "redecorating."

"I was heartbroken," Tom admits.

Upset though he was, Tom was relieved and proud to hear his name finally called by the Patriots. It meant he would have an opportunity to realize his childhood dream. Rather than wallow in disappointment, Tom immediately focused his energy on proving wrong all those who doubted him. He not only wanted to *make* the Pats—he resolved that one day he would become the team's starter.

By the time Tom reported for training camp in August he had already committed the New England playbook to memory. Tom's teammates had seen a lot of rookies come and go, but never had they seen one arrive so thoroughly

Did You Know?

The first time Tom removed his shirt in the Patriots' locker room, his teammates could not stop laughing. They had never seen a skinnier NFL player.

prepared. Little did anyone realize, but Tom was laying the foundation for all the amazing things to come.

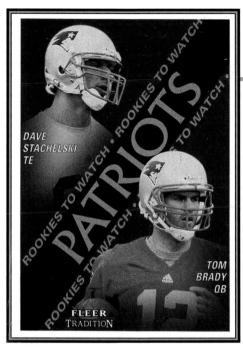

Tom shared his Fleer rookie card with Dave Stachelski, a fifth-round pick who failed to make the team.

As an NFL fourth-stringer, there was no chance Tom would see any serious playing time in 2000. In his mind that was a good thing. Tom's primary goal was to win the back-up job in 2001, and he would need at least a year on the sidelines to do that. He would also need a year in the workout room. Tom's legs and upper body needed a lot more muscle.

What Tom saw from the sidelines in 2000 was not pretty. The Patriots had some very good players, but they were a bad football team. They finished last in their division with a 5–11 record. Tom's only appearance came at the end of a 34–9 loss to the Detroit Lions. He completed one pass for 6 yards. Still, one big positive came out of this lost season: Tom no longer had any doubt he could play in the NFL.

"There weren't any surprises," he says. "The way I looked at it, I'd been playing with pro football players at Michigan. Brian Griese, Charles Woodson, Tim Biakabatuka—we had a lot of guys who went to the pros from Michigan. I'd played with them there. Why couldn't I play with them here?"

"Drew Bledsoe was the New England Patriots. That's what I grew up watching, thinking."
—TOM BRADY

*Despite completing just one pass in 2000, Tom felt he was
ready for anything heading into 2001.*

Looking Like A Leader

"Even when he wasn't number one or number two, there was something about him that made guys notice."

—TEAMMATE DAMIEN WOODY

The same New England Patriots who teased Tom about his spindly build in 2000 were in awe of his new physique when he reported for camp in 2001. His legs were stronger, his chest was rippling, and his arms and shoulders looked like bands of steel. He was still the skinniest guy on the team, but he had packed on a good 15 pounds (6.8 kg) of quarterbacking muscle. As soon as the Patriots hit the practice field they saw the difference this made. With the same easy motion he used to drill 10- to 15-yard passes, Tom was now zinging the ball 30 yards downfield.

Though Tom looked sharp in training camp, no one could have guessed he would have his own SI FOR KIDS card a few months later.

Tom had also assumed something of a leadership role—rare for a bench-warmer who had seen little action in his lone NFL campaign. During the off-season, Tom had taken unofficial charge of team workouts, just as he had in high school. Also, when camp opened, Tom made sure things were going smoothly for all the first- and second-year players, and alerted the coaching staff when he sensed any problems with the young guys.

After practices, Tom would corner team veterans and ask them questions about their positions. He quizzed the linemen, runners, receivers, and even some of the defensive players. Tom's goal was to know every player's responsibility on every play. Quarterbacks coach Dick Rehbein was a tremendous help in this department. He was Coach Belichick's most popular assistant, and he had taken Tom under his wing the year before.

A couple of weeks into training camp, Rehbein died of a heart attack. Word of the coach's passing devastated the team. Coach Belichick gave his players several days to deal with the loss, then asked them to regroup and get back to work.

Did You Know?

Tom was a perfect 60-for-60 in on-time attendance at training camp during the summer of 2001. His reward was a choice parking spot for his yellow Jeep Wrangler.

Tom felt the best way to honor his fallen friend was to take what he taught him and move a step closer to the starter's job. John Friesz had moved on, which left Tom in a three-way battle with Michael Bishop and Damon Huard. When practice resumed, Tom bumped his game up a notch. The Patriots released Bishop and told Tom he was the team's new number-two signal-caller.

The promotion meant the world to Tom, but it barely made the newspapers in New England. The football writers covering the team were predicting another gloomy season for the Patriots. In their eyes, the club had failed to address its most glaring deficiencies, which included the running game, the receiving corps, and the defense. The coaching staff begged to differ. During the off-season, the Patriots had signed several free agents to address these problems. None of the new players was a "big name," but Coach Belichick believed that they were the kind of veterans who would do their jobs well, and this in turn would make the other players that much more effective.

Among these new New Englanders were cornerback Terrell Buckley, linebackers Roman Phifer and Mike Vrabel, running back Antowain Smith, and receiver David

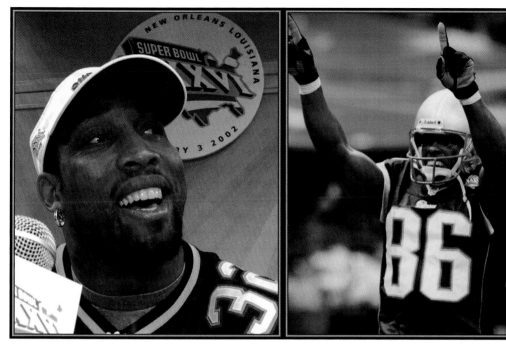

Antowain Smith (left) and David Patten (right)—two of the key pickups made by the Patriots in 2001.

Patten. The team also drafted defensive tackle Richard Seymour and offensive guard Matt Light. They were the types of rookies who might make an immediate difference.

The rest of the team was pretty much as it had been the year before. Bledsoe's offensive line was anchored by guard Mike Compton and center Damien Woody, who was quick off the ball and could handle most defensive tackles one-on-one. On defense, mercurial Bryan Cox and dependable Ted Johnson led the linebackers, while cornerback Ty Law could cover any receiver in the league. Safety Lawyer Milloy was one of the most underrated players in football. His solid skills and superior instincts made him the linchpin of New England's complicated defense. The special teams were good, too. Troy Brown, a speedy punt returner who could slash through the slimmest openings, gave New England a potential game-breaker. Kicker Adam Vinatieri, a holdover from New England's last Super Bowl team in 1996, had a strong leg and nerves of steel.

Player-by-player, it may not have been an impressive group. But almost every starter brought some exceptional quality to the field. It was the kind of team that could find a dozen ways to beat you . . . or a dozen ways to beat themselves. The experts claimed it

Drew Bledsoe takes a pounding against the Jets. He would leave the game with a life-threatening injury.

was the same old story: The Patriots would go only as far as their superstar, Bledsoe, would take them. Most of the preseason magazines picked the Pats to finish last in their division.

The team took a step in this direction in the season opener, losing to the woeful Cincinnati Bengals, 23–17. The Bengals manhandled the Patriots in the trenches, and burned them through the air. Bledsoe had his usual good game, completing 22 of 38 passes, but the defense could not contain Corey Dillon and Darnay Scott, Cincinnati's two main weapons.

The team played better against the New York Jets in the season's second game, but trailed with five minutes to go in the fourth quarter. Bledsoe had been in this position before and beaten the Jets. New York knew this, and increased its pressure on the quarterback whenever he dropped back to pass. On one play, Bledsoe was pursued all the way to the sideline by linebacker Mo Lewis, who blasted him out of bounds.

Bledsoe was no stranger to rough tackles, but this one felt a little different. He shook off the pain and went back into the huddle, but moments later he had to come out. Tom went into the game and drove the team down to the 29-yard line, but could not get the ball in the end zone. The final gun sounded and the Patriots were now 0–2. Worse, Bledsoe's injury was very serious. The Lewis hit had actually sheared a blood vessel in his chest, causing internal bleeding. Had Bledsoe not gone to the hospital right away, he could have died. The veteran would be out at least two weeks, doctors predicted, and possibly much longer.

Tom Brady was now the team's starting quarterback.

The Brady Bunch

chapter 6

> "Brady is a guy the players
> can really rally around."
> —**BRIAN BALDINGER, TV ANALYST**

The question on everyone's lips heading into week three was: "Who is Tom Brady?" Coach Belichick's job was to educate fans and the press. "Tom has a good arm and a good head on his shoulders," said the New England coach. "He is hard-working and confident, but certainly not overbearing. The team, both players and coaches, have confidence in him. He has backed that up through his performance on the field, both in college and as a professional. He is very consistent on a daily basis. It's not just a flashy play here or there. He is a

"Inexperienced quarterbacks need to show they can deal with the highs and lows of this league. Tom proved he can deal with it."
—**OFFENSIVE COORDINATOR CHARLIE WEIS**

Tom gets a high five from Drew Bledsoe after producing his first touchdown as a starter.

consistent player—one who, the more you are around him, the more he grows on you."

Belichick did not say what New Englanders were hoping to hear, that Tom was a budding superstar, or that the team would be just as good with him in the lineup. In truth, the coach had no idea how Tom would do. No backup in the league knew his job better, and Belichick had never had a player more prepared for this type of opportunity. Still, in the heat of battle anything can happen, and the coaching staff was secretly preparing for the worst.

Tom faced the Indianapolis Colts in his first game as a starter. Their high-powered offense had already scored 87 points in two games, but the Colt defense was also prone to giving up points. The New England defense pulled together to force several key turnovers, while Tom played cautiously in a 23–13 win. Reality set in a week later, however, when the Miami Dolphins trounced the Patriots, 30–10. Tom was even more conservative in this game. He tried so hard to limit his mistakes that he missed opportunities to make big plays. Also, the leadership skills he had displayed in camp were absent in the huddle.

Sensing that their season might be slipping away, Lawyer Milloy approached Tom after the game and told him the team needed a more dynamic leader. Drew Bledsoe was quiet and laid back, which was fine. But Tom had been loud and lively during camp. Where *was* that guy? Milloy told him to take charge—his teammates would gladly follow.

The twenty-four-year-old heeded the veteran's advice. All week long Tom practiced with the confidence and gung-ho attitude that had been missing in the first two games. It paid off at crunch time during Sunday's game. The San Diego Chargers held a 10-point lead with less than four minutes to play. Tom drove the Patriots to two scores to tie the game, then set up Adam Vinatieri's game-winning field goal. Afterward, Tom's teammates began to realize they might have a very special quarterback on their hands.

The Patriots played the Colts next, and once again Tom made the difference. He threw for three touchdowns in a 38–17 blowout, including a 91-yard scoring strike to David Patten. This play not only broke a team record for the longest touchdown pass, it also showed Tom's teammates that he could improvise under pressure. Originally, a different receiver's number had been called, but Tom glimpsed Patten blowing past his man and hit him with a perfect pass. The touchdown also sent notice to the league that Patten was for real—he was fast, and he could be dangerous in single coverage. With

former All-Pro wideout Terry Glenn having a disappointing season, this was a real boost to New England's fortunes.

Tom had won three of four games in Bledsoe's absence, and his personality had won over the team. Belichick and his staff saw the Patriots put

David Patten reaches for a pass from Tom during New England's December victory against the Jets.

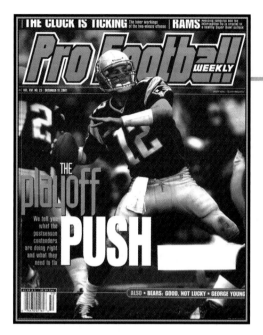

Tom makes the cover of PRO FOOTBALL WEEKLY. *Ten weeks earlier no one had heard of him.*

out an effort for Tom that wasn't always there when Bledsoe was calling the shots. It would make for an interesting decision when their star was fully mended.

In a week seven duel with former Michigan teammate Brian Griese, Tom faltered against the Denver Broncos. He was looking good until the fourth quarter, when the Denver defense started using alignments he had never seen before. Four interceptions later, the Patriots walked off the field 31–20 losers. It was a good lesson for Tom, and a reminder to the rest of the team that he was inexperienced. However, the following week, Tom surprised everyone by bouncing back with a masterful game against the Atlanta Falcons. He threw for 250 yards and 3 touchdowns to lead the team to a 24–10 win. When reporters asked Tom what the difference was, he was quick to credit Bledsoe, who was still on the mend. He had spotted a flaw in the Atlanta secondary and helped Tom exploit it all day. When Tom beat the Buffalo Bills, 21–11, in the next game, New England had a winning record for the first time all year.

The season's biggest test was next. The St. Louis Rams, the most talented team in the NFL, came to Foxboro Stadium. Quarterback Kurt Warner, running back Marshall Faulk, and receiver Isaac Bruce would give the New England defense all it could handle. Pass rushers Leonard Little and Grant Wistrom would be in Tom's face all day, while Aeneas Williams would patrol the defensive backfield for the Rams.

Tom did a good job of keeping the Rams off-balance by passing when they expected a run, and handing off when they expected him to pass. In fact, the Patriots looked to have the game under control until Antowain Smith fumbled near the St. Louis goal line. The Rams marched the ball 97 yards for a score and never looked back. They won a tight, well-played game, 24–17.

The Patriots had been winning games by keeping the score close and then forcing turnovers. They were unable to accomplish this against the Rams, but felt good about the rest of their performance. In the season's remaining six contests, the team was able to execute its game plan to perfection in wins over the Saints, Jets, Browns, Bills, Dolphins, and Panthers to finish with an 11–5 record—the opposite of the previous year's mark. Although Bledsoe had gotten back into playing shape, Coach Belichick stuck with Tom as the starter the rest of the way.

The coach's reasoning was perfectly logical. By the time Bledsoe was healthy, New England had gone 6–3 under Tom, and team chemistry had never been better. The offensive line was playing far beyond expectations, Smith had rejuvenated his career in the backfield, and the receiving corps had really clicked with Tom.

Bledsoe was unhappy with the decision to keep him on the bench. There is an unwritten rule in the NFL that says a quarterback cannot lose his job to injury. When he is healthy, he should get a chance to win it back. Under almost any other circumstances, Bledsoe would have gotten that chance. But the team was just playing too well to make the change. In the first game after this controversy started brewing, Tom led the Patriots to a 17–16 comeback victory against the Jets—their most important win

of the season. Three weeks later, New England hosted Miami in a game that likely would decide the division championship. The defense made a game-turning play and Tom showed great maturity in the face of a relentless Miami pass rush. The Pats beat the Dolphins, 20–13.

Tom looks like an old pro against the Panthers in the final game of the regular season.

Walking the Fine Line

"Before, you were kind of the new kid on the block. It's not as much the case anymore."

— TOM BRADY

The Patriots were scheduled to host the Oakland Raiders in their first playoff game. Although no American Football Conference (AFC) team had distinguished itself as a true Super Bowl contender, many experts believed the Raiders had the best postseason squad. Veteran quarterback Rich Gannon had enjoyed a marvelous season, the team's running attack was deep and dangerous, and receivers Tim Brown and Jerry Rice were as frightening a duo as any the Patriots had faced.

At kickoff, a steady snow was falling over Foxboro Stadium. This seemed to favor the Raiders in the first half. Their defense did a great job against Tom and his teammates, while the Oakland offense put 7 points on the board. The Raiders added a field goal in the second half and held a 10–0 lead heading into the fourth quarter. Tom rallied his troops, capping off a scoring drive by diving across the goal line himself.

Tom, flanked by Raiders Greg Biekert and Charles Woodson, watches helplessly as the ball skids away. Fortunately for the Patriots, the play was ruled an incomplete pass instead of a fumble.

With the score 13–10, the Patriots got the ball back with one last chance to keep their season alive.

There is a fine line between winning and losing in the NFL, especially in the play-offs. Often the difference is a single play. Sometimes it even comes down to an official's call. Of course, this was the farthest thing from Tom's mind as he coolly maneuvered the team into Oakland territory with time ticking away. He still needed to complete a long pass to get the ball into Adam Vinatieri's kicking range.

Then came the play fans will be debating for years to come. Tom dropped back into the pocket and scanned the field for an open receiver. Just as he was preparing to throw, Charles Woodson—his old Michigan teammate—reached out and knocked the ball to the slushy turf. The Raiders pounced on the loose football and began celebrating their victory.

But not so fast. Referee Walt Coleman had whistled the play an incomplete pass. He knew that Tom always patted the ball once before he threw, and consequently this was considered part of his throwing motion. Since Woodson had jarred the ball loose

Tom is helped to the bench after spraining his ankle in the AFC championship game.

while Tom was patting it, technically he had begun his throw—and thus the correct call was an incomplete pass, not a fumble. After checking the replay, the decision was upheld and the Patriots were awarded the ball.

Tom made excellent use of this second chance, moving the ball to the 28-yard line. Vinatieri came on the field and split the uprights to tie the game. In overtime, Tom was as good as he had been all year. He completed eight straight passes before giving way to Vinatieri, who hit from 23 yards to win the game. Afterward, Tom credited his stunning overtime performance to the coaching staff, which advised him to run the team's special no-huddle two-minute offense. "Earlier in the game I was seeing a lot of defen-

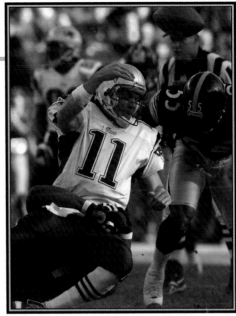

The Steelers batter Drew Bledsoe, who subbed for Tom in the title game. Bledsoe held on for a 24–17 win.

sive looks," Tom says. "But once we went to the no-huddle, they [the Raiders] only had three or four calls, and I knew what to expect."

The Patriots moved on to the AFC championship game against the Pittsburgh Steelers. Once again, New England was cast as the underdog. But the Steelers were also something of a surprise. The previous week they had defeated the defending Super Bowl champs, the Baltimore Ravens, in convincing fashion. The experts considered this game a "toss-up."

Unfortunately for the Patriots, it was *Tom* who got tossed up by the Pittsburgh pass rush. Late in the second quarter, he hit the turf hard and sprained his ankle. Drew Bledsoe came in, hit David Patten with a touchdown pass, and then nursed New England's lead right through the second half for a 24–17 win. The Patriots were going to the Super Bowl, and Tom was on cloud nine.

Once the euphoria wore off, the Patriots faced the grim reality of the job that lay ahead. Their opponent in the big game would be the St. Louis Rams, a team that had gotten stronger since their first meeting, and was now firing on all cylinders. Oddsmakers favored the Rams by as much as three touchdowns, meaning the Patriots were bigger underdogs than any team in the previous 35 Super Bowls. Looking back, it seems preposterous. But man for man, the Rams were indeed far better than the Patriots. And it certainly did not help that Tom's ankle was still painful and swollen.

In the days leading up to the game, two questions were on everyone's mind: How badly would St. Louis destroy New England, and who would Coach Belichick choose as his starting quarterback?

Although Tom had not even taken the practice field, there was no question in *his* mind who would start. "When you get to this point, you can't miss a game like this," he told reporters. "I don't anticipate not playing. The hypothetical of not playing really doesn't enter my mind."

*Tom and Coach Belichick
hold a sideline strategy session.*

When New England fans were polled on this question, they were split. They loved and admired Tom for all he had done, but Bledsoe was the healthier of the two, and he had been to the Super Bowl before. It was definitely a tough choice, but the man who had to make it knew all along who his starter would be. The moment Tom's ankle looked steady, Coach Belichick told the world that Brady would start the game.

In truth, Belichick was far more concerned with the *other* team's quarterback than his own. Kurt Warner posed all kinds of problems for the New England defense. He was a strong and accurate passer who could choose from four excellent receivers. If the secondary paid too much attention to these pass-catchers, it would open things up for Marshall Faulk, who could run the ball around end or up the middle when he wasn't hauling in Warner's tosses for big gains.

The Patriots' defensive coaches devised a game plan around the thing that had gotten them to the big game: limiting mistakes and creating turnovers. To do this against the Rams, the defense would have to wear them down by hitting hard on every single play. Only then would St. Louis' timing be disrupted enough for the Patriots to make their "big play."

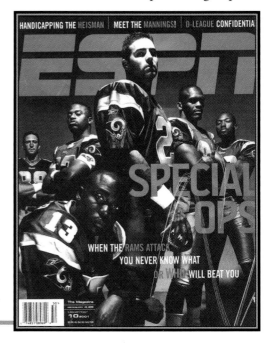

*The Rams looked scary on this
magazine cover, but that was nothing
compared with how they looked on the field!*

Patriots Day

chapter 8

> "You can't say
> enough about the kid."
> —TEAMMATE DAVID PATTEN

The New England Patriots had looked to their young leader to set the tone throughout the season. Now, in the hours before the scheduled kickoff of Super Bowl XXXVI, they wondered whether Tom Brady would be upbeat or nervous. He was neither. In fact, when they looked for Tom they found him asleep on the training table. The veterans got quite a kick out of this. Talk about calm! "I'd never really done that before," Tom smiles.

When the teams finally sprinted onto the field, the emotion pulsating through the Louisiana Superdome put a charge into the Patriots. From the moment the game started, the New England players seemed a split-second quicker and a lot meaner than their opponents. Every time one of the St. Louis stars got near the football, at least two Patriots dropped him with a vicious hit. The Ram defense

Bobby Hamilton executes New England's game plan to perfection, dragging Kurt Warner.

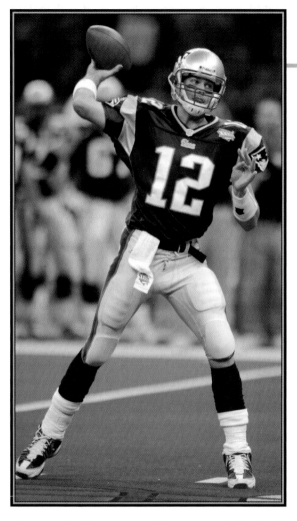

Tom spots David Patten in the end zone at the end of the first half. His scoring strike gave the Pats a 14-3 lead.

was performing well, too, but the flavor of this game was playing right into New England's hands.

Midway through the second quarter, with St. Louis ahead 3–0, Kurt Warner dropped back to pass with linebacker Mike Vrabel hot on his trail. Warner attempted a short throw, but Vrabel hit his hand as he followed through. The ball wobbled through the air and Ty Law picked it off. The New England cornerback pranced 47 yards into the end zone. Warner left the field clutching his hand in pain. He would not be the same player for the rest of the day.

With time running out in the second half and a 7–3 lead, Tom got the ball and marched the team downfield. The Rams were starting to panic, and Tom knew it. He called a play that sent the speedy Patten streaking toward the back of the end zone. Ball and receiver arrived together for a beautiful touchdown. The Patriots went into the locker room up 14–3.

During halftime, Coach Belichick praised his players for their perfect execution of the game plan. Then he reminded them that, across the hall, the St. Louis brain trust was busy making adjustments. The Rams, he assured them, would not go quietly. Despite an 11-point lead, the Patriots could expect the fight of their lives in the second half.

And that is exactly what they got. The Patriots managed a third-quarter field goal, but otherwise the Rams kept them under wraps. The St. Louis line held the Patriots defense at bay, while the Rams defenders stalled Tom's offense. In the fourth quarter,

Tom gets perfect pass protection during Super Bowl XXXVI. New England's surprising performance against the Rams was a total team effort.

Warner drove the Rams deep into New England territory and carried the ball across the goal line himself to cut the deficit to 16–10. With just under two minutes left, Warner made another clutch play, hitting Ricky Proehl with a super touchdown pass. Jeff Wilkins booted the extra point to knot the score at 17–17.

"As soon as Proehl went into the end zone, I asked, 'What are we doing?'" Tom remembers.

He was told they were going for it. "That's exactly what I was hoping we'd do," Tom says. "Drew came over, Damon Huard came over. We talked about some things that might work."

Wilkins kicked off and after a short return, Tom took the field with 1 minute 21 seconds left. Pinned back on the 17-yard line, the New England offense seemingly had nowhere to go. Everyone, St. Louis included, believed the Patriots would simply run out the clock and regroup in overtime. Tom caught the Rams by surprise with a pair of short passes to running back J.R. Redmon, which gave the Patriots a first down on their

Adam Vinatieri launches the winning kick against the Rams.
New England's victory is considered the greatest upset in Super Bowl history.

own 30-yard line. After an incomplete pass, Tom hit Redmon again with an 11-yarder for another first down. There were now only 41 seconds left.

Tom stopped the clock with an incompletion, then threaded the needle to Troy Brown on a crossing pattern that moved the ball into St. Louis territory. Tight end Jermaine Wiggins snagged a 6-yard pass before being tackled at the Rams' 30-yard line, and Tom rushed up to the line of scrimmage to take a snap and spike the ball to stop the clock. There were seven seconds left—enough for one more play.

Tom trotted off the field, his heart pounding, his eyes wide. He had just done the impossible. Now it was up to the cat-cool Vinatieri to split the uprights and win the game. Tom held his breath with the rest of New England as the ball left Vinatieri's shoe and sailed end-over-end beyond the outstretched arms of the St. Louis defenders and through the goal posts for a 20–17 victory.

It was a game like so many others New England had won in 2001. But this one was different. This was the Super Bowl. The Patriots had just pulled off one of the great upsets in football history, and they had a world championship to show for it.

No Longer A Nobody

chapter 9

"My biggest fear is to
end up being a one-hit wonder."
—TOM BRADY

om Brady went from football obscurity to sports immortality in the course of four months. By all accounts, it could not have happened to a nicer guy. Tom was the heart of the Patriots throughout their miraculous championship year, and he was at the center of the celebration when his teammates streamed onto the field in New Orleans to exult in their Super Bowl win. Much like the man himself, his final numbers were modest—just 16 completions for 145 yards. Nevertheless, Tom was named Super Bowl XXXVI Most Valuable Player.

Tom's life was a whirlwind after the Super Bowl. After telling the world he was "going to Disney World" during the postgame celebration, he actually showed up in Orlando the very next day, and rode down the theme park's Main Street with

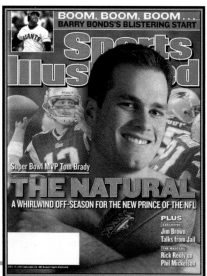

It's not often that two superstars from the same high school share the same SPORTS ILLUSTRATED cover!

Tom waves to the crowd in Boston during the team's victory parade.

Mickey Mouse. He hopped a plane and rejoined the team for their welcome-home party in Boston, where fans lined the streets to hail their conquering heroes. Tom got the biggest cheers of anyone.

Next on Tom's travel itinerary was a trip to Hawaii to play in the Pro Bowl, where more accolades came his way. While on the big island he also got in a round of golf with former NFL great John Elway. On his return trip, Tom stopped for a few days in Arizona, where he met two of his idols, Barry Bonds and Willie Mays, at the San Francisco Giants' spring training complex. Bonds, coming off a record-smashing 73-home-run season, could not help noting that he was now the second most famous alumnus of Junipero Serra High!

A few days later, Tom was at a charity function, sparring playfully with Muhammad Ali. He also served as a judge in the 2002 Miss USA pageant. Exhausted, Tom had to start turning down invitations, including one for the Academy Awards. He also politely asked San Mateo officials to postpone plans for a "Tom Brady Day" until he had a chance to catch his breath. Tom was discovering that the aches and pains of a football season were nothing compared with the brutal schedule of a media superstar.

"I'm trying to learn as I go along," he says. "I think I'm a pretty good quarterback, but there's all this other stuff that goes along with being a very recognizable person, and I suck at it. This is my new reality, I guess, and it's knocking me down."

Tom eventually turned his focus to the coming season. He knows that in sports, the pressure to follow a great year with another great year can be intense. If you don't, well,

Tom's easy style and supreme confidence remind some of the late John Unitas, another quarterback who "came out of nowhere" to become a champion.

you are considered a "flash in the pan." Everyone will be gunning for Tom and the Patriots now, which means they have to be better than ever.

Tom knows this, and he is determined not to let his celebrity get in the way of his football. "Why do so many guys have one great year and then play so badly the next?" he asks. "Well, now I know why—because there are so many things that can take you away from what you need to do to focus on your job. I've really got to live up to my end of the bargain, and I've got to play like a Pro Bowl quarterback, every week, every day in practice."

In the months following New England's championship, the team made some important moves. The Patriots added speed and depth and gave Tom more receivers to work with. And Drew Bledsoe was traded to the Bills, ending any question as to who the Patriots' number-one quarterback is.

The team looks to Tom for different things than it did from Bledsoe. Whereas Bledsoe was expected to "carry" the offense, Tom is being asked to "manage" it. He will do so with an impressive array of weapons. Tom has established himself as one of the

pro stats

Season	Team	G	Att	Comp	Comp %	Yds	TDs
2000	Patriots	1	3	1	33.3	6	0
2001	Patriots	15	413	264	63.9	2,843	18
Total		16	416	265	63.7	2,849	18

pro achievements

Pro Bowl Selection 2001
Super Bowl XXXVI MVP 2002

NFL's best short-yardage passers, reading defenses rapidly and choosing his receivers with great intelligence. He can throw the long ball when he needs to, but his real skill is to make quick gains on first down, which takes enemy defenses out of their game plan. Tom's weaknesses are his speed and footwork—a good pass rush can still tangle him up. Needless to say, that is one of the things he is always working on.

Of course, the connection between preparation and success is nothing new to Tom. If anything, the success he has enjoyed has just made him want to work harder.

"Look, I'm a football player," he says. "When I think back on all the cool stuff I've done, the most fun I've had by far was winning the Super Bowl. There are so many distractions that can make you lose sight of what's important. Well, the heck with that. I know how I got here, and I'm going to devote myself to helping my team win it all again."

"The great thing about Tom is that no matter what he went through, it didn't seem like he allowed the pressure to bother him. A lot of guys might have reacted to the big stage of the Super Bowl by trying to force plays, but he just relaxed. Right now he seems like a kid in a candy store."
—KURT WARNER

Tom says he will never lose sight of what's important in football.

Index